Fixing
Broken Glass

A collection of poetry and journal entries

Written by Conee Berdera

For the person I once loved

May our love remain in these pages. A bittersweet memory that will bloom in each chapter.

Table of Contents

CHAPTER I

The Art of Falling

"Lovers don't finally meet somewhere. They're in each other all along."

— <u>Rumi</u>

The Beginning

A shake of thunder beneath this steady chest.

As the universe spilled these colors,

These eyes gazed at this fragile passion, without rest.

This is where it starts.

Lover you are the chorus.

You found your way into my heart.

Skin Deep

My mother's condescending friend offers the worst advice. She happily tells me that the only way I could get a boyfriend was if I 'lost all this weight'. She grins at me like it was a compliment. As if her statement would save me from all misery.

In her defense she thought this was encouragement. Because what the heck, she cannot imagine anyone loving a fat girl.

Though I remained silent. I gulped the hurt. I let it sink silently underneath my skin. I remind myself this is not the first time my body has been ridiculed.

I bit my tongue.

A mix anger and disgust filled my heart. I wanted to throw her a punch. Instead, I sighed.

I knew that I had a body large enough to be a boulder. Because whenever I entered the room, the crowd parted like the Red Sea.

My body may never be the ideal. Yet I wonder if she knew that I felt at home here. How this was never a prison; but a place of solace.

My anger then faded. The rage now transformed to pity. This is when I realized she never saw love like I did. She did not know the courage it took to love myself when the entire world told me not to.

She did not know my lover's story. How it went beyond the size of my body. How it was an affair of the soul. How our love defied everyone's prejudice.

I soon left the party.

I met my lover at their doorway. We embraced like it was the last night of the world. And I realized that I am such a lucky girl.

For we loved each other beyond all reason. And I guess not all knew love like this.

Masterpiece

I have fallen in love with poems, paintings and songs. But it is true indeed my love, you are the most beautiful art form of all.

Concealed

There is a girl who loves you.

She will never have the courage to say anything.

But her heart is slowly slipping into your fingertips.

So, she fills her journal with love letters she will never send you.

Each poem is a eulogy for a boy she can never love.

Innocence

I miss the girl I used to be; like her eyes that spoke of innocence and her mind that was full of wonder. But of all things, I miss her heart the most. The heart that loved ferociously without a hint of fear. A heart that loved so greatly the universe could burst in tears. How pure and unblemished. For she was a girl who has never been hurt. Carrying a heart that was pure love to the fullest sense. How I wish I could love that way again.

By All Means

Darling how the longing pulls the strings tighter. As the world keeps us at a painful distance. I will skip across continents, as my feet feel sharper across the Earth. For I will cross oceans by using my skin as a raft. And no matter how the moon pulls the tides, I would safely float back to your doorstep. Because we both know, I would do anything for you.

Let Go

She chased love like a child trying to catch a butterfly.

Her heart was left in the dirt, covered in scratches.

Her eyes stung from all the crying.

For she realized her foolishness.

How she tried to reach the sky for someone who never loved her in the first place.

Gentleness

He taught me how love can be soft. How he ignored his brother's rage towards anything fragile. Believe me. He showed me how a man can love; soft, fragile, not of afraid sinking his walls underneath the vast waters.

Fusion

You slowly became a part of me.

For we were two branches grafted in good measure.

How our souls interlaced deep into the earth.

Our minds rushed in rivers of joy.

Our hearts deeply rooted in love.

Our bodies merging into one.

Our arms hoping never to let go.

Us

We are twilight. The connection where day and night do not separate. Even if the world wants them to.

Algorithms

The odds weren't always in my favor. The statistics of my past relationships has ordained love to be the main symbol of destruction. For the outcome shall be another broken promise. Another collection of tears. Yet out of my foolishness I am building steps around you. As we walk together; I hope this will not end in heartache.

Reading The Body

My body was a book full of poetry, and your lips
just brought all my words to life.

Calypso

I guess the Olympians thought they could break you.

But you are a woman of great strength.

You have spent thousands of years in utter solitude.

Every single lover that came never chose to stay.

But you loved freely anyway.

You built him a ship for his voyage back home.

Made sure he was in the safest hands, when you guided the very winds to send him away.

You leave me baffled.

How can someone love so much, yet expect nothing back?

The Farthest String Attached

The short time we spend near each other, frustrates my heart like I could burst. Despite the great distance that tries to pry us, my heart still follows you to the ends of the Earth.

Quarantine

The pestilence may drift me further away.

Hands are now behind a screen.

Embraces are messages thrown into the ocean.

How touching your face again feels impossible; like a distant memory in which I shall no longer wake.

So my mornings count the endless days.

Because this love will not end in tragedy.

This is just a chapter.

The beginning of something wonderful.

For I am here.

You are still safe with me.

Intoxication

I haven't had a drink for about a year. But I find it so hard to stay sober now. For his kisses leave me breathless. As my cheeks flush in an utter state of elation. My body feels so drunk I can barely keep my thoughts together. My heart is merry in my dreams of forever. Yet if we part ways, I would dread the hangover.

Cherish

Loving you

was like holding

the most valuable light

within my hands.

So fragile and beautiful it was.

Yet I also feared the day

it might slip through my fingertips;

one by one

or all at once.

Apparition

I bask in another mirror.

I read another selection of books.

What I once lost, I have found once more.

Lovely it is, yet it terrifies me to the core.

I swore to give up.

To darken this ink black.

To appear blind in everything I was holding back.

Yet I am sinking back into the love I swore to never rekindle.

The love falls in too deep for me.

I can no longer hold on to the act,

for my heart renames itself fickle.

Generations

I fold over words pressed neatly underneath my bed. It was a Sunday and all I can I think about is this.

I am exhumed from a century of sleeping.

How I was given prophecy that you would find your way back.

When I lulled myself to sleep, each dream was about my past life.

Each century was another confirmation.

When you resurrected every hope I had for love.

Now a generation of heartbreak does not matter. My grandmother's tears do not look like my own. How droplets slowly fill a vase until it is full.

This Time

I promise to love you like I've never heard my own heart shatter before.

Labels

You clearly believed in labels. For your bedroom was excruciatingly organized; each corner everything was alphabetically arranged in labeled boxes. And I noticed that you had a name for everything. As I found myself wrapped around your arms, I questioned what my name meant within your heart.

"What am I?" I said.

"My girlfriend," you replied.

Beloved

The anguish of heartbreak has forgotten the woman that you are.

Breathe.

The seasons are changing yet you are loved.

Breathe,

The arms around you are no longer his.

But the heavens still adore you.

Breathe,

You're the Mona Lisa in your own right.

The belladonna at the very heart of the forest.

Swim across the ocean.

Remember how you are flesh and bone birthed from their very chest.

Breathe,

How you are never a missing piece.

So let all this salty air remind you that you are worthy.

Let the waves dry each wound.

Kiss your own scars.

You were always worthy even before they came here.

Breathe,

remember how the heavens still adore you.

Breathe,

You were always good enough

.

The Forest of Unrequited Love

Unrequited love is this bittersweet tragedy. How the heart just wants something it can never have. Like how a tree bows down to the roaring winds. How the tree breaks down before it. How it gives everything to the wind. How it says "Take everything for I will love you always,". Yet the wind whispers back after the storm. And the wind says sorrowfully "I'm so sorry I can never love you in this way. But I am forever grateful for this,". And the crestfallen tree still stayed.

Soulmates

It is the calm of the heart

while the oceans sink you deeper.

It is finding the other part Zeus cut from you.

It is kindness and understanding intertwining souls.

And of course, it is your shape.

It is your brain.

It is your soul.

It is you

I love you for who you are

She Deserved Better

On the nights his loneliness stings him harder than cheap liquor; he suddenly thinks of her. For he revels in the memory of her heart placed on his hands. As he tried to get drunk on other people's skin. Yet all that regret still burns his chest. And now he realized that he once had the best. Since she loved his highs and lows. He thought about what he once held. He regrets leaving her. But the girl now loves somebody else, a boy who loved her for being herself.

Grey

I wonder why are we so afraid of love? How it baffles me that humanity fears the very thing that is needed for it to survive.

Brushing Palms

I will never forget the first time we held hands. The soft touch of our palms. The uncertainty relieved with our fingers locked together. My stomach bursting with butterflies. It was something so underrated yet so gentle, so perfect and so powerful. Funny how starlight was brought forth by two imperfect hands. For holding your hand felt like holding your soul.

Philophobia

Have you ever feared love after getting hurt? How you assumed that everyone who moved your heart was eventually destined to break it.

The Last Time

I was so drunk on every word you uttered. 'I love you,' you said. As you softly caressed my cheek. My heart fluttered with so much delight. Yet I paused with wonder.

For when was the last time you told someone else the exact same thing?

Spellbound

As he flicked his pen across each page, the boy brought forth another galaxy of stars. For his poetry brought so much more music to my lips. And I wonder, if he realizes just how beautiful he is?

Allure

Loving you felt like I finally had direction. It was like your soul was the center of gravity, and my heart ran all the way to you.

Naked

My greatest moment of intimacy, was not the evening we took all our clothes off. But it was when you saw me at my most difficult state. Like how you witnessed the most unlovable parts of me. As I slowly unraveled each imperfection in front of you like a scar. And despite all of this, you loved me harder anyway.

The Act of Loving

All the love I ever gave would always come back to me. However, I would not always receive it from the people I gave it to.

Honesty

You're my favorite chapter of my story. You've read the dark pages and smiled at the joyful ones. And you found me beautiful; while you kissed my scars away in the dark. For you made realize what love really was; the act of loving someone for who they really are.

I Love You

On her worst days I just held her. I know my love won't cure her depression. But I wanted her to know that she will never fight alone.

The Heart of The Sea

The ocean always reminds me of love. The vast body of majestic beauty. How it leaves me feeling at awe. How the shore kissing me with waves reminds me that there are deeper waters. One where your heart is afraid to fall in too deep. Yet it is still able to push itself up to the shore. Then once you're in dry land, you'll ask yourself "When will I ever love this way again?".

December

December was the month of realization for me. You see, your body was a home of warmth. How we crawled inside each other. For I felt so safe whenever you wrapped your arms around me. And no matter the cold; I felt warm indeed. For I'm so blessed that someone like you, loves someone like me.

Whenever We Love

When love shows up, we hold on to it so tight.

It is something we can't really let go of

without a fight.

How it colors everything with beautiful delight.

For we claim to hold it forever if we do right.

But when love told us to let go,

we couldn't help but cry.

So when 'love' finds us again

 we grip our hearts so tight.

While our minds pray for 'forever' this time.

For we find solace in believing that this 'love',
won't end in a goodbye.

The Last Time

I was so drunk on every word you uttered. 'I love you,' you said. As you softly caressed my cheek. My heart fluttered with so much delight. Yet I paused with wonder.

For when was the last time you told someone else the exact same thing?

By All Means

Darling how the longing pulls the strings tighter. As the world keeps us at a painful distance. I will skip across continents, as my feet feel sharper across the Earth. For I will cross oceans by using my skin as a raft. And no matter how the moon pulls the tides, I would safely float back to your doorstep. Because we both know, I would do anything for you.

Reading the Body

My body was a book full of poetry, and your lips just brought all my words to life.

Intoxication

I haven't had a drink for about a year. But I find it so hard to stay sober now. For his kisses leave me breathless. As my cheeks flush in an utter state of elation. My body feels so drunk I can barely keep my thoughts together. My heart is merry in my dreams of forever. If we part ways, I would dread the hangover.

CHAPTER II

The Downfall

"Ever has it been that love knows not its own depth until the hour of separation."
— **Kahlil Gibran**

Infidelity

I still love you so much.

But I cannot fathom how you broke me.

How you swore I was your entire world,

yet at the same time you destroyed mine.

Breaking Point

"Please don't leave," he said. I tried my best to stay but my heart could only take so much. His tears were rolling down his face. Like a child I tried to make things light. I cracked a few jokes. For I just wanted him to smile again, even for the slightest second. But he ended up giving me a half-meant smirk. So, I grabbed my things out the door. And I definitely knew this was goodbye.

But before I left the porch, I stared into his eyes. A pool of sorrow I will forever recognize. As I left he had one last appeal for me. And with a heavy heart I looked at him. "I will always love you," he said. I soon saw my tears kiss the floor. I slowly walked away from him. "I'm sorry," he said. He picked up his heart and left. Then at the airport, I wondered if I made the right choice.

Fraud

I am doing the right thing.

Why does this feel wrong?

My heart will recover from the damage you left.

Why do I feel like I can't fix it?

I no longer love you.

Why am I lying to myself?

Deafening

Your name was once the loveliest note that caressed my ears. But now, your name is the saddest sound I hear.

Secrets

You're a young soul that is pure fire. Yet you are also the calm sea; a set of eyes that lead me back home. You're also the favorite chapter of my story. You have embraced me for who I am. And you cherished me despite that I'm this wounded girl. This melancholic soul. This broken piece. You have accepted the terrible and beautiful parts of me. But my beloved best friend, will you ever know? Yet the secret will hold itself too close to you. I've have always dearly loved you so.

The Dividing Line

I would let you

take my heart once more.

Even if you'd break it

for the hundredth time.

And yet...

A part of me stays firm.

Because sometimes

love isn't a good enough

reason to stay.

New Eyes

I poured the wine up to the brim of my glass. I choked in the tears, the regrets.

I've held another lover in my bedroom. I've spread my flesh apart hoping the warmth

will numb out this agony.

But self-destruction cannot bring me closure,

 nor the new lover sleeping next to me.

"I am the only one who can fix myself," I sighed.

Yet the epiphany left me sobbing the entire night.

 But I slowly saw everything in a brighter

light.

Your love makes me face what I refuse to see. I hate you for making me want something that cannot be.

   -I feel it now

Melancholy

I reached out for another hand to wipe these tears;

 used someone else's warmth to cover my skin. I've set myself on fire just to burn so easily next to him. Then it hits me. *Loneliness* isn't *love.*

Drowning

I wrote down all my sorrow.

I tossed it straight into the ocean.

I kept hoping it would not emerge from the depth.

I kept praying his memory would sink deeper.

Because I knew that he never once thought of me.

That felt so much deeper than the sea.

Grief

I guess our story placed pain on our footsteps. Bruised our hearts to bleed all over the ground. How the tender flesh of our souls were pierced with sorrow. Our blood gently trickled on the solution we never found.

The Music Box

We no longer speak.

But my heart

silently sings you a lullaby.

It serenades you sweetly across the night sky.

It whispers blessings underneath your ear.

Yet it is only the moon that can hear.

Transparency

Think this over for me. You claim to see my beauty, my kindness, and my resilience. Yet, are you sure that you love me? For you have not seen my scars my dear. I am an imperfect woman. Amongst all the starlight I hold is a bouquet of thorns you have not seen yet. My fragility is my greatest strength and weakness.

So when you claim to love me; ask yourself 'Do you really?'. Do not utter the word 'love' too quickly. 'Love' has lost its meaning. Do not play with it across your tongue. For it is a divine gift. It has birthed art, life and colors into the universe. Do not utter it, if your heart gives an insult to its existence.

Luna

'You remind me of the moon,' he said. For in this world of darkness, she was full of luminescence. The way the center of his soul was connected to her so strongly. That even the moon and the roaring tides were made jealous by the sight of them. Yet unlike the moon pulling towards the ocean, their love sank deeper as if there were no end. And when they were far apart, the tides made sure their hearts would always find each other again.

Here's Why

You went after me despite the fact my parents hated you. I remember how your embrace felt like going home. And our fingers interlaced as you whispered the sweet letters that our mouths etched into. We were the young lovers kissing under a rainstorm.

Our love was like the first bloom of spring. Your warmth revealed another side of my heart. And we came forth together like the first sprout growing through the snow.

I noticed that you meant every word you said. So I joyfully gave you my heart.

But years later, everything changed. "I love you" was something you used to tell me every day. Yet now you never showed it. It sounded like a broken record. Maybe it was me. Maybe it was you. Maybe I just assumed you were telling the truth. "I love you" is kind of overused. Like the time you said I was the only one, but you had another girl, thinking she was the only one too.

Yet despite a few 'I love you's' you would always make me cry my eyes out. And the world that looked warm and red suddenly seemed cold and blue. For I gave you every piece of my heart and I stayed true. Yet you broke me like I meant nothing to you.

So now I realized that it was only my heart telling the truth. But sometimes we pretend that we don't see the truth in order to drown out the hurt. We assume the hurt is okay because we'd rather feel this way than lose each other. But I'm sorry. Loving you is a storm I can no longer partake in.

So cease the lie that you love me. Because I love myself enough to say that I deserve better than tears and a broken heart. I wish you all the best, but I'm sorry. This is the chapter where I have to stop loving you, even if I don't want to.

Alone

Despite the crowd, the friends, the neighbors…

I feel lonely. A painful strike of solitude across my heart. I'm never alone, yet I feel solitary. Like a heart longing to be understood. And I greatly wonder why? *How can such silence roar so loud?*

Just Like That

I always fought for him. Yet he never once fought for me. And I just felt like a shield he threw into the sea.

The Foolish Martyr

It was so stupid but I guess the most painful part about this is the fact that you said you 'loved me'. How you made me feel special. How you held me around your arms. How you made fall for you in a single kiss on the mouth.

 I turned into something desperately in love with you. And in a split second you broke me. And you stood there marveled. That this girl would take a bullet for you, even if you're the one holding the trigger.

Atlantis

You have left footprints on each chapter. And sometimes my heart feels like a lost city. How everything has sunken deep, leaving remnants of a love that is now lost.

Reluctance

You just stopped caring. And just like that we went from soulmates to strangers.

Shipwreck

the hallways lull

 a siren's song of heartache.

Our arms reached out for mending.

Like misplaced puzzle pieces

gradually losing its parts.

Our feet slowly sinking into the water.

Our fingertips slowly pulling apart

Presumptions

He makes me feel like I am the most valuable person in the world. Yet I remind myself that I cannot assume that he 'loves' me.

Remnants

The harsh reality is;

I still love you.

I will always love you.

I just learned how to survive without you.

Aphrodite's Lament

Funny isn't it? How these mortals love others so easily, yet some of them cannot even love themselves.

Now

Back then we held each other's hearts like it was the most fragile thing our hands could touch. How our love was the softest surface to grace us. Yet here we are now. The years have pulled as farther. How we no longer speak. How the wreckage left us full of sorrow and longing. Our hearts torn yet still so in love.

Regrets

If only I told you that I loved you.

If only I told you that you were my favorite best friend.

If only I had the strength to tell you how I felt about you.

I know you would've loved me back or turned away my heart.

But you would never doubt that you meant the world to me.

And I would not be here regretting everything I could have told you.

I wish I could utter another 'I love you' right before you disappeared. As you embraced her at the other side of the world.

For I just somehow wish you were here.

If only…

This Is A Haunting

My love for him was a ghost. A memory that could not see the light. His faced showed up in moments that I didn't want to check. His eyes lingered on my head as I kissed my different lovers. And during my unguarded moments my feelings for him came back to haunt me.

Listen

The start of healing is when you acknowledge the pain.

A Prayer for My Heart

I realized that I cannot unlove you. So now my heart has a new prayer. I pray that you'll find happiness. And in return, I will find mine. I pray that someone will love me the way I loved you. And may I love this person a thousand-fold more than you. By then I'm sure my heart will stop looking for you.

Fisherman's Wound

Today I saw him move on. He placed his heart on the lap of another woman. He whispered every single 'I love you,' into her ear. And I stood there elated for him. Grinning at his new-found happiness. But deep down I still cry. For my love for him was always fisherman's wound. The great pain heals anyway. But the wound stings like a ghost coming to haunt me.

Photographs

Everything we once had.

Only so much can remain,

yet one by one the images start to fade.

Transparency

Think this over for me. You claim to see my beauty, my kindness, and my resilience. Yet, are you sure that you love me? For you have not seen my scars my dear. I am an imperfect woman. Amongst all the starlight I hold is a bouquet of thorns you have not seen yet. My fragility is my greatest strength and weakness.

So when you claim to love me; ask yourself 'Do you really?'. Do not utter the word 'love' too quickly. 'Love' has lost its meaning. Do not play with it across your tongue. For it is a divine gift. It has birthed art, life and colors into the universe. Do not utter it, if your heart gives an insult to its meaning.

Surrender

I saw how our mistakes drew the poison straight out of our tongues. When our faces stared at the rubble, we realized what has succumbed. But...

The ink drips faster than my tears.

I see how the story ends.

Our worlds will shatter beside us.

Yet even after the war,

our love never left the battlefield.

Grief

I guess our story placed pain on our footsteps. Bruised our hearts to bleed all over the ground. How the tender flesh of our souls was pierced with sorrow. Our blood gently trickled on the solution we never found.

Amends

A bottle of all the tears I have caused you.

A box of all the gifts you have given me.

A book of apologies.

Believe me.

I never meant to hurt you.

The Rain Dance

Perhaps I feel the pain rummage. My heart now settles within all this ache. The clouds curl into a darker phase. When the rain pours out graciously; the flowers lovingly receive the drops.

The people in the village dance underneath its massive shower. The children giggle as they go puddle jumping.

 I soon run into the storm; I splash along. Joy then greets me at the street. She runs to kiss my bruising heart.

'Sorrow has left' she said.

 I began to celebrate for the mourning has stopped, and joy was the only thing my heart had to offer.

Resilience

My life is a forest of sorrow. But I see the gentle rays of joy pass through the foliage. I run aimlessly through the trees; hoping it is a pathway to happiness.

Secrets

You're a young soul that is pure fire. Yet you are also the calm sea; a set of eyes that lead me back home. You're also the favorite chapter of my story. You have embraced me for who I am. And you cherished me despite that I'm this wounded girl. This melancholic soul. This broken piece. You have accepted the terrible and beautiful parts of me. But my beloved best friend, will you ever know? Yet the secret will hold itself too close to you. I've have always dearly loved you.

Deafening

Your name was once the loveliest note that caressed my ears. But now, your name is the saddest sound I hear.

Melancholy

I reached out for another hand to wipe these tears;

 used someone else's warmth to cover my skin.

I've set myself on fire just to burn so easily next to him.

Then it hits me.

 Loneliness isn't *love.*

Drowning

I wrote down all my sorrow.

I tossed it straight into the ocean.

I kept hoping it would not emerge from the depth.

I kept praying his memory would sink deeper.

Because I knew that he never once thought of me.

That felt so much deeper than the sea.

Memories

Sometimes solitude haunts your soul like an abandoned house. How you feed on this bittersweet longing, whenever you wait for a love that will never come back for you.

The Music Box

We no longer speak.

But my heart

silently sings you a lullaby.

It serenades you sweetly across the night sky.

It whispers blessings underneath your ear.

Yet it is only the moon that can hear.

Thoughts on Giving Too Much

But I guess you made me realize that I had just so much love to give.

And I know you aren't to blame,

for we cannot control those who fall for us.

But my heart is a roaring ocean.

How it burnt passion across me like a flame.

How it burst into a billion stars when it found you.

For I gave you every inch of myself.

How I offered you my universe,

as you softly traced your fingers across the stars.

How you worshiped the moon yet you never called her 'yours'.

And I still gave you everything, even if you never loved me back.

The Dividing Line

You asked for another chance.

I held on to the phone sobbing; tumbled in a mix of emotions. A bittersweet ache it was for you to comeback.

How I would hold you closer to me.

That I would let you take my heart once more.

Even if you'd break it for the hundredth time.

And yet...

A part of me stays firm.

Because sometimes

love isn't a good enough

reason to stay.

CHAPTER III

Recovery

The wound is the place where the Light enters you."
— **Rumi**

Before and After

I recall the force of magic

that drew me to you.

The softness of your skin.

The soft whispers of love.

Yet now...

We are on opposite ends.

A reminder that sometimes

amazing things

will somehow

come to an ending.

There is Beauty in What's Temporary

Usually, when someone says something won't last forever, it's associated with something negative. But there is beauty in what is temporary.

Headaches and stressful nights do not last forever. Traffic does not last forever. Itchy mosquito bites don't last too. And fortunately, the hurt goes the same way. The heartbreak you feel now whether they left you, you left them or when they never wanted you in the first place.

This state of brokenness isn't eternal. The scars they left you can fade.

Like the moment he left me when my body was useless for him. The tears you cried will not always be of sorrow. This will not last forever.

The ache, the pain, and the anger are just a season. Something fleeting. Your heart will sing a new song. And it will no longer ache like this.

So, stand up, catch your breath. You need to continue living. You will smile again. I promise you. I promise you will love again. You will dance again to a new song. So please enjoy this tragically beautiful thing we call life. And your heart will beat to another song as you dance to the music. You will fall in love with moments that are beautiful. Your migraine will go away. And you'll definitely love a lot better.

There is such beauty in things that are not eternal. The constant gift of eternal change is maddeningly breathtaking. Just watch the beauty of life evolve right in front of you and enjoy every single moment of it. I promise you. You will definitely smile again.

The Rose

My dear remember this:

You're strong.

You're important.

You're loved.

You can make it.

For your life is a beautiful bud slowly blooming.

Please keep living to see the seasons of your life

in all its beautiful glory.

How it slowly emerges out of the thorns.

Revealing the lovely flower.

Life is worth living it.

Please keep doing so.

Recovery Takes Time

Every heart heals differently. So just take it a day at a time my friend. You'll soon see your heart laughing again.

You Were Always Complete

A lover is a blessing. But remember my dear, a lover can never complete you. They are not the missing piece of your soul. They are also not the measure of your worth. So if you ever find yourself alone; remember that you were always whole to begin with.

Reconciliation

For years, I have resented my body.

Pierced my soul with daggers of insults.

All for the fact I could not fit the mold they wanted
my shape to be.

So I ended my cycle of hatred.

Then my soul held my body around her.

Pressed her lips on my ear as she whispered

"I am sorry'"

"I love you,"

"I accept you,"

"You are perfect the way you are,".

My body cried.

For she was the house

my soul was looking for all this time.

The Princess Stopped Waiting

She stopped looking for her other half. For she realized she was whole. Unblemished nor lacking, she was imperfect perfection itself. She blamelessly loved herself on her own. Another person's love was just another jewel to the crown she held. *The only love she needed the most was from herself.*

You Can Do It

I'm proud of myself today. Though I feel such melancholy, I have the courage to stay alive. So I gladly take pride. And I've made it this far. Thus, I remind myself 'If I can survive today, I can survive tomorrow'.

To My Best Friends

Wonderful isn't it? Like how the universe brought us together. How our friendship seems like a beautiful accident. A peculiar chance of meeting. How a person so similar yet so different can mirror my soul. And though sometimes our lovers come and go; a best friend is there for you through it all.

I Wish You Nothing But The Best

My heart was a home we once lived in. Even after you left me, it still had so much space for you.

Soon I dreaded the fact that I still held you dearly. How I tried to remove you like a stain. Washing off its remnants like soap. Yet, my life still had your mark. For how could I forget the moments we shared when I loved you for several years?

I realized that I will always love you. Even when my heart heals and loves another. You will still hold a special place. Because back then, you held my hand in the dark, wiped my tears as I cried, kissed my lips like glowing starlight, kept all my secrets as I showed you my scars. This showed that you did love me once.

But I still believe that we crossed paths for a reason. And I know that I will find my own happiness in return. For my heart is an overflowing garden. All this love will someday be shared with another. How it will bloom with every lesson we learned. As my next lover thrives in the soil of my heart. It will be a beautiful garden; full of the love you left behind.So

I now pray that you will find happiness. I pray that you fall in love again. And when you do, I hope she loves you more than I ever did. Please make her feel loved each day. The same way you did for me. So that she may know the wonderful man that you are. As I now wish you the best.

There is Always Hope

I know that today is hard. But my dear you have to be brave. Though you may not feel like it sometimes; life is a gift that is definitely worth it. So please continue to keep living it. You're worth so much love and respect. Please never forget that.

Notes After a Breakup

I'm moving on; as I miss you less and less each day. I soon realized my home was always within myself. For I will always be complete despite the damage you left me. So I guess this tragic goodbye taught me how to love myself more. Like the way I chose to be better, even if I'm on my own this time around.

Freedom

The most beautiful and liberating love story I have ever seen and felt; it was when I finally learned to love myself.

Acknowledgments

This book would have not been possible without my good friend Juansen Dizon. Thank you for inspiring me to write.

I also send my gratitude to Jonathan Meyer and Christi Steyn for sharing my work on social media.

Last but not the least, I will like to give thanks to my best friends Jed, Bea and Ace. Your unconditional love has sought me through thick and thin. I love you all so dearly.

About The Author

Conee Berdera is a writer and spoken word artist based in Manila Philippines. Her work has been featured in multiple digital magazines such as Thought Catalog. If she is not writing you can find her gardening with her dog Kobe.

Made in the USA
Columbia, SC
21 November 2021

49251009R00069